Don,

I hope you enjoy
reading these daily,
as you remember
God made you to
live like a king's kid,
a prince of
the king of kings!

God bless,
Ramona

HIS
BATTLE

HIS
BATTLE

GOD'S PLAN FOR VICTORY

JACOB A. SHEPHERD
WITH SHERI ROSE SHEPHERD

Revell
a division of Baker Publishing Group
Grand Rapids, Michigan

Published by Revell
a division of Baker Publishing Group
P.O. Box 6287, Grand Rapids, MI 49516-6287
www.revellbooks.com

Printed in Singapore

ISBN 978-0-8007-1923-4

10 11 12 13 14 15 16   7 6 5 4 3 2 1

Lance Cpl. Randy L. Newman
MAY 25, 1985–AUGUST 20, 2006
"A strong and valiant warrior"

I have fought the good fight,
I have finished the race,
and I have remained faithful.

2 Timothy 4:7

Contents

A NOTE TO THE READER
FROM JAKE SHEPHERD

As a fellow follower of Christ, a seeker of the truth, and a man chasing after the heart of God, I have found it is never easy to stay on the right path. It seems that around every corner there is something waiting to hinder us from running the race the Lord has set for us. In fact, it seems to me that the harder I push after God, the harder the enemy pushes back against me. Often I have found myself discouraged, disoriented, tired, and ready to quit.

I'm sure you have felt the same way at one point or another in your life. Maybe you are there now. Every man who has ever sought after God has felt lost and discouraged, has suffered defeat, and has seen dark times and seemingly hopeless situations. But in the end, the man who perseveres also sees victories won, wounds healed, relationships mended, and lives restored. And he experiences the powerful, forgiving love of the Father.

It is my hope that this book will help you experience encouragement and love from your heavenly Father on a personal level. It is my hope that the intercessory prayers I offer in this book will help refresh you, renew your mind, and transform you. I hope you will be encouraged in your desire to become a righteous man of action, one who chooses life and recognizes all the blessings your Father has placed before you. I hope and pray that you will find yourself better able to stand strong for a heavenly standard of living and that you will be a man who overflows with the perfect love of God.

I trust you will be open and able to apply the letters and prayers in this book to your life, wherever you are. And I trust that you will let God's Holy Spirit lovingly convict and correct you and mold you into a man after God's own heart.

May God bless you and keep you fighting the good fight.

A NOTE TO THE READER
FROM SHERI ROSE SHEPHERD

A few years ago I was waiting to catch a plane at the Atlanta airport. I glanced across the room and saw a young soldier waiting for his flight. His face was filled with fear and uncertainty, and it was clear that he was being deported to war. Having a mother's heart, I had to walk over and attempt to bring the young man comfort and encouragement.

As we began to talk, he shared how hard it was to say good-bye to his family and how heartbroken his mom was that he was leaving. I opened my bag and handed him my book *His Princess Love Letters*, and I told him to give it to his mom. He thanked me. I prayed with him, said good-bye, and went back to my own seat. To my surprise I watched him open the book and begin to read. Then I saw tears rolling down his cheeks.

After a few minutes, the young man walked back to me and said, "Ma'am, we men need a book like this in our own language." At that moment, I asked the Lord for a book that would strengthen and encourage men the way my *His Princess* books have for women.

I have three men in my life I consider heroes: my dad Phil, my husband Steve, and my son Jake. Over the years, I have observed their lives and have seen their deep desires to keep their faith, fight for their families, and conquer something great in their lifetimes. At the same time, life hits them hard as men sometimes, and that hero's heart gets lost for a while. But I have witnessed firsthand how the power of prayer and the truth of God's

Word have given each of them the strength to get back up from their fears and failures and keep fighting to finish strong.

These three men are my heroes, not because they are perfect, but because they have allowed the Lord to painfully prepare them for greatness through tough times. I believe that God created men with a good kind of fight inside them, and my three men have never quit fighting, especially for their loved ones.

That prayer I prayed, asking God for a book for men like my three heroes—men young and old who are searching for God's strength, wisdom, and truth—was indeed answered. The Lord in His faithfulness gave me this book's vision, and my son Jake caught the vision with me from his man's point of view. Today it is our honor to present *His Battle* to men.

May each of these letters and intercessory prayers encourage and equip you to win any battle you face. As you read, may guilt be replaced with grace, and may pain be turned into renewed passion. You are chosen by God. May you find the strength and wisdom through these readings and prayers to keep your faith, fight the good fight, and finish strong.

All God's best for you.

He trains my hands for battle;
    he strengthens my arm to draw a bronze
      bow.
You have given me your shield of victory.
    Your right hand supports me;
    your help has made me great.

Psalm 18:34–35

TOGETHER THEY WILL BE LIKE
MIGHTY WARRIORS IN BATTLE
TRAMPLING THEIR ENEMY INTO
THE MUD OF THE STREETS.
THEY WILL FIGHT BECAUSE THE
LORD IS WITH THEM,
AND THEY WILL PUT THE ENEMY
HORSEMEN TO SHAME.

ZECHARIAH 10:5 TNIV

THE FRONT LINE

My Son,

You were born to become a hero. There is a deep desire inside your soul to conquer something great. I know this because I placed it there. The only thing holding you back is you. Don't hide behind your fears and insecurities any longer. There is a fight in your heart, which wants to be on the battlefield. This fight is not just for you; it is for all those you love. I need you to willingly walk to the front line. Don't look back any longer, but look forward to the great victory that lies ahead of you. I will give you the same strength and courage I gave to King David over Goliath. All you have to do is step out in faith.

Your Lord,
who fights for you

BE STRONG AND LET US FIGHT BRAVELY FOR
OUR PEOPLE AND THE CITIES OF OUR GOD. THE
LORD WILL DO WHAT IS GOOD IN HIS SIGHT.
....

2 SAMUEL 10:12 NIV

Dear Brother,

I pray you will have the courage and the
strength to be the one who fights when no one
else can. May you reflect the glory of your
Father's faithfulness by leading others into
battle and defeating the enemy. I pray that
you will wield the divine power the Lord has
equipped you with and that you will trample
Satan under your feet by the authority of the
name of Jesus. May you have vision to see
beyond a circumstance to the victory and
freedom on the other side. I pray blessing and
strength over you.

In Jesus' name,
Amen

PREPARE FOR BATTLE

My Son,

The time is now—get dressed for battle.
I have not called you to a life of comfort.
When you feel as if there is no fight left inside
you, call Me and you will feel My Spirit rise
up inside your soul and give you strength. I
alone hold the passion you need to persevere
in any battle. I am your strength when you
are weak. In My power you will conquer any
spiritual giant that attempts to defeat you.
Put on every piece of spiritual armor that I
have given to you, and bury your heart in My
Word. Your life will not be wasted when you
fight to further My kingdom. I have already
given you victory . . . now take it!

Your King,
  who shields you

Therefore, put on every piece of God's armor so you will be able to resist the enemy in the time of evil. Then after the battle you will still be standing firm. Stand your ground, putting on the belt of truth and the body armor of God's righteousness . . . and take the sword of the Spirit, which is the word of God.

EPHESIANS 6:13–14, 17

Dear Brother,

I pray you will cover yourself with the glorious armor of the Lord and fight this good fight. I pray you will keep yourself protected under His love and be victorious over every attack, never backing down until the battle is won. May you crush the enemy under your feet in the name of Jesus. May all darkness flee as you walk in the light of the Lord. I pray you remember that the Lord is for you; therefore, no one can stand against you. Go in the power of the Spirit and walk in Him to victory.

In Jesus' name,
  Amen

He put on righteousness as his body armor
And placed the helmet of
salvation on his head.
He clothed himself with a
robe of vengeance
And wrapped himself in a
cloak of divine passion.

ISAIAH 59:17

Then if my people who are called by my name will humble themselves and pray and seek my face and turn from their wicked ways, I will hear from heaven and will forgive their sins and restore their land.

2 CHRONICLES 7:14

THE POWER OF PRAYER

My Son,

Never underestimate the power I have given you in your prayers. You have the same power inside of you that I gave Elijah to call down fire from heaven and reignite faith in the hearts of men. I want you to confidently call on heaven so you may see My mighty hand move on earth. Your words spoken in someone's dark hour will move My Spirit to light their path. Your prayer for the lost and lonely will usher in My Spirit to comfort them and send My angels to their aid. One day, on the other side of eternity, you will see how your prayers affected and protected many lives during your life.

Your God,
  who loves when you pray

And I will do whatever you ask in my name, so that the Son may bring glory to the Father. You may ask me for anything in my name, and I will do it.

JOHN 14:13–14 NIV

Dear Brother,

I pray you will now, more than ever, know the power you hold in being chosen of the Most High. You have been given the ear of the King of Kings. Whatever you ask, He is there to give it in His love. I pray you will take this weapon and use it regularly. I pray that you will be filled with the power and conviction of His Spirit and that you will be an unstoppable force of prayer for His people in these dark times. I pray you will see mountains moved, seas parted, and the sick healed in the name of Jesus. I pray you will never doubt His promise that He hears the cries of His people and does not ignore them.

In Jesus' name,

Amen

My Son,

You no longer have to be controlled by circumstances; you can learn to live your life fueled by faith. What you see will cause you to lose hope, but your faith will free you from fear and give you the power to persevere through trials. If you have faith even as small as a mustard seed, I will move any mountain that stands in your way. With faith, nothing will be impossible for you to accomplish. But I cannot force you to have faith in Me. Only you can make the choice to believe. If you choose to stand on My Word, you will see My promises come to pass in you and through you.

Your King,
  who has faith in you

I TELL YOU THE TRUTH, IF YOU HAVE FAITH
AS SMALL AS A MUSTARD SEED, YOU CAN
SAY TO THIS MOUNTAIN, "MOVE FROM
HERE TO THERE" AND IT WILL MOVE.
NOTHING WILL BE IMPOSSIBLE FOR YOU.

MATTHEW 17:20 NIV

Dear Brother,

I pray your faith will be increased with every
new day and every new trial that comes your
way. May you never forget all the times in the
past that your Savior has pulled you through
the darkness. He will never leave you. He is
always faithful. I pray, in the name of Jesus,
that you will not be shaken by any doubts or
insecurities or trials the enemy tries to throw
at you, because you have placed your faith
in Christ. I pray you will never find yourself
doubting your Creator. He holds the world
in His hands, and He sees you as His faithful
warrior.

In Jesus' name,
Amen

NOW FAITH IS THE SUBSTANCE OF THINGS HOPED
FOR, THE EVIDENCE OF THINGS NOT SEEN.

HEBREWS 11:1 NKJV

Don't you realize that in a race everyone runs, but only one person gets the prize? So run to win! All athletes are disciplined in their training. They do it to win a prize that will fade away, but we do it for an eternal prize.

1 CORINTHIANS 9:24–25

My Son,

It is time for you to discipline yourself spiritually the same way an athlete trains to win a race. I know what I ask of you is not easy; however, your perseverance will make you the great man I created you to be and will bring glory to Me. Don't waste your race running for the praises of people. You must run this race of faith keeping your eyes fixed on the eternal prize I will give you when you cross the finish line. You will never look back with regret if you let Me, your Life Coach, push you to your full potential. You will do more than run; you will win!

Your Lord,
  your Life Coach

*Therefore, since we are surrounded by such
a great cloud of witnesses, let us throw off
everything that hinders and the sin that
so easily entangles, and let us run with
perseverance the race marked out for us.*

HEBREWS 12:1 NIV

Dear Brother,

I pray you will not grow tired or weary of the race that is set before you. You have been designed by God to succeed and to fulfill a calling that is yours and no one else's. I pray you will throw aside every weight and sin that would so easily entangle you and slow you down. In the name of Jesus, you will run in the freedom and power that has been given to you by His great sacrifice. You are more than a conqueror in Jesus, and I pray that you will strive for the excellence you have been called to and that you will succeed. May the witness of your life glorify the Lord.

In Jesus' name,
Amen

BUT IN MY DISTRESS I CRIED OUT TO THE LORD;

YES, I PRAYED TO MY GOD FOR HELP.

HE HEARD ME FROM HIS SANCTUARY;

MY CRY TO HIM REACHED HIS EARS.

....

PSALM 18:6

My Son,

When life hits hard, I suffer with you. I, your Savior, know the burdens placed upon you, because I have already carried them on My shoulders. In My darkest hour I was alone, and I cried to My Father for another way—a less painful way. Yet I chose to walk this path of pain for you. Just as olives must be crushed to make oil, I poured out My life as a love offering for you. Don't give up your faith in these dark hours. There is powerful purpose in your suffering. I hear your cry for help, and I will come to your aid. I am your Rock and Rescuer, and I will deliver you.

Your Lord,
  who suffers with you

HE WILL ONCE AGAIN FILL YOUR

MOUTH WITH LAUGHTER

AND YOUR LIPS WITH SHOUTS OF JOY.

....

JOB 8:21

Dear Brother,

I pray that in the middle of your suffering and brokenness, you will find Christ in His fullness. May you feel Him carry you through and trust Him to use these trials to build in you perfect endurance for the race ahead. I pray you will find peace knowing that the Creator of the universe hears your prayers, rescues His children, and works everything together for your good. May you be overcome with the joy of the Lord and rise above your circumstances to see what your heavenly Father sees for your life.

In Jesus' name,
Amen

My Son,

It is critical that you shield your mind with truth and be strategic about what you allow yourself to read, watch, and even think. The enemy will try to invade your mind with every sinful thought. His goal is to cripple your calling by setting tempting traps. Do not allow the enemy's sensual weapons to destroy the man I destined you to be. Every evil deed is first constructed in the heart with one thought. Run from whatever thought weakens your walk with Me. You can take control of your thoughts by immersing yourself in My Word. Victory is yours . . . walk in it.

Your Savior,
  who gives you victory

*We demolish arguments and
every pretension that sets itself
up against the knowledge of God,
and we take captive every thought
to make it obedient to Christ.*

2 CORINTHIANS 10:5 NIV

Dear Brother,

I pray you will take every thought captive and submit it to your Father. Only He can give you true peace of mind. May you dwell on the things of the Lord. May His kindness, love, and mercy leave no room in your heart or mind for things that are not of Him. I pray you will remember to cover your mind with the helmet of salvation that Jesus gave you through His death on the cross and His resurrection. May you not be polluted or distracted by anything that does not bring you into His presence. May you fill yourself with His truth, believe it, and keep your mind sanctified.

In Jesus' name,
Amen

Finally, brothers, whatever is true,
whatever is noble, whatever is right,
whatever is pure, whatever is lovely,
whatever is admirable—if anything
is excellent or praiseworthy—
think about such things.

PHILIPPIANS 4:8 NIV

He will declare to his friends, "I sinned and twisted the truth, but it was not worth it. God rescued me from the grave, and now my life is filled with light."

JOB 33:27–28

My Son,

I know you live in a world that believes many
lies. But I have equipped you to fight the
temptation to live a lie. You know who I am,
and I am the truth. Anything that does not
line up with My Word is a lie. I want you to
become radical for My truth. I know there
will be times when truth will be a tough road
to travel, but it is the only road that keeps you
free from walking in guilt and condemnation.
It is only My truth that helps the lost find
their way to Me. Live for My truth and throw
off any lies that have been placed on you. Discover the freedom that is yours to share.

Your King,
   who is the truth

Who may worship in your sanctuary, LORD?
Who may enter your presence
on your holy hill?
Those who lead blameless lives
and do what is right,
speaking the truth from sincere hearts.

PSALM 15:1–2

Dear Brother,

I pray you will be a seeker of the truth. May
you find peace only on the path the Lord
has created for you to travel. May you live in
the truth of who your heavenly Father says
you are so you can ignore the lies this world
throws at you. You are a child of the Most
High God. He has set you apart and created
you exactly how He wants you to be. I pray
that your confidence in His truth will never
fade and that your example will bring others
to a new, full life in Christ.

In Jesus' name,
Amen

My Son,

This is not the time to surrender to the immorality and wickedness of this world. You are much needed on the battlefield. No weapon formed against you can or will destroy you, because you are Mine. You have the power in My name to demolish anything the devil uses to attack you. Don't fight using the weapons of the world. Make up your mind to fight in My power, and take authority where I have given you authority. This is your time; take your shield of faith and use it to protect yourself and those who don't know how to protect themselves.

Your Commander and King,
who fights for you

FOR THOUGH WE LIVE IN THE WORLD, WE DO NOT WAGE WAR AS THE WORLD DOES. THE WEAPONS WE FIGHT WITH ARE NOT THE WEAPONS OF THE WORLD. ON THE CONTRARY, THEY HAVE DIVINE POWER TO DEMOLISH STRONGHOLDS.

2 CORINTHIANS 10:3–4 NIV

Dear Brother,

I pray you will not let yourself be destroyed
by the feeble attempts the enemy uses to try
to bring you down. May you have faith that
your God is so much bigger than anything
that can come against you. May you fight
strongly with the weapons He has freely given
you. I pray that you will not cower but that
in Jesus' name you will refute and destroy
any foul words or actions that try to stop you
from being all your Father created you to be.
May you be blessed and victorious in battle.

In Jesus' name,
Amen

"NO WEAPON FORGED AGAINST YOU WILL
PREVAIL, AND YOU WILL REFUTE EVERY TONGUE
THAT ACCUSES YOU. THIS IS THE HERITAGE OF
THE SERVANTS OF THE LORD, AND THIS IS THEIR
VINDICATION FROM ME," DECLARES THE LORD.

ISAIAH 54:17 NIV

Do not be afraid of the terrors of the night, nor the arrow that flies in the day. Do not dread the disease that stalks in darkness, nor the disaster that strikes at midday. Though a thousand fall at your side, though ten thousand are dying around you, these evils will not touch you.

PSALM 91:5–7

BECOME FEARLESS

My Son,

I have not given you a spirit of fear but of a
sound mind. I have not called you to run away
from the battles this life brings but to face
the giants in your life and to conquer them.
As long as you walk in My power and truth
and you surrender your conflicts to Me, you
have nothing to be afraid of. Therefore, I call
you fearless, the way I called My chosen one
Gideon a valiant warrior when he was afraid
to fight. Do not be disheartened by what your
natural eye sees. I am the same God who gave
Gideon the power to overcome his enemies,
and I am fighting for you right now. So I command you, as your King, do not fear.

Your God,
   who demolishes fear

Make the LORD *of Heaven's*
Armies holy in your life.
He is the one you should fear.
He is the one who should
make you tremble.
He will keep you safe.

ISAIAH 8:13–14

Dear Brother,

I pray you will walk in the perfect love of
Jesus Christ, in which there is no fear. May
you realize that God desires you to be a brave
man after His heart. Spend time with Him to
refuel your courage. Know that nothing is too
big or too frightening for the Lord. May you
find your confidence in your heavenly Father
and your peace in His Son. May you fearlessly
face and overcome any enemy in the name of
Jesus. I pray you will hold fast to this truth
that nothing can come against you when you
are safely in His arms.

In Jesus' name,
Amen

THEREFORE, IF ANYONE IS IN CHRIST, HE IS A

NEW CREATION; OLD THINGS HAVE PASSED AWAY;

BEHOLD, ALL THINGS HAVE BECOME NEW.

....

2 CORINTHIANS 5:17 NKJV

My Son,

Real courage is exemplified when you willingly let go of who you are now so you can
become who I have called you to be. Your
courage to humble yourself and confess
your sin to Me will become the key to your
freedom. You will find something far greater
than temporary pleasures. You will discover a
powerful peace unlike anything this world has
to offer. I gave My life for you to have a better
one. I will also give you courage to walk away
from the old ways and embrace your new life
in Me. You are Mine, and I call you by name.
Take the power I have given to you and make
a change!

Your King,
  your courage

IF WE CONFESS OUR SINS, HE IS FAITHFUL
AND JUST TO FORGIVE US OUR SINS AND TO
CLEANSE US FROM ALL UNRIGHTEOUSNESS.
....

1 JOHN 1:9 NKJV

Dear Brother,

I pray you will be encouraged to change by the grace and love your heavenly Father has extended to you. May you be compelled by His goodness to turn from sin and walk into the life He has for you that is full of peace and joy. May you know God's redeeming love and His restoring power, and may they be a testimony to everyone you meet. I pray that once you change, you will never go back to your old ways but you will see how precious you are to the body of Christ. May you embrace your new life in Him.

In Jesus' name,
Amen

GET UP

My Son,

One of the greatest battles you may ever face is the fight to forgive yourself. I have already forgiven you and empowered you. I gave My disciple Peter the strength to get up from the guilt of denying My Son Jesus. I gave My appointed king David the grace to get up from the shame of committing adultery and murder. I gave My apostle Paul the mercy to get up from the horrors of persecuting My disciples. I gave My warrior Gideon the courage to get up from his fears and lack of self-worth. I am asking you to receive whatever you need from Me, to accept My forgiveness, and to get up and finish strong.

Your King,
  who helps you up whenever you fall

Even if godly people fall down seven times,
they always get up.

....

PROVERBS 24:16 NIrV

Dear Brother,

I pray you might know and accept the wonderful grace of God. May you find restoration in His unconditional love and forgiveness. I pray, in the name of Jesus, that you will no longer feel needless guilt or shame. His Son has already paid the price for anything and everything you have done or will do. I pray that you will not be held captive by the condemnation of the enemy but that you will be set free by the truth of who your Father says you are. May you take the hand of your Savior and let Him lift you up and place you where you are supposed to be.

In Jesus' name,
Amen

Do not remember the former things, nor consider the things of old. Behold, I will do a new thing, now it shall spring forth!

ISAIAH 43:18–19 NKJV

Refrain from anger and turn from wrath;
do not fret—it leads only to evil. For
evil men will be cut off, but those who
hope in the LORD will inherit the land.

PSALM 37:8–9 NIV

THE BAIT OF BITTERNESS

My Son,

I know how hard it is to react righteously when feelings of anger hit your heart. I felt every emotion you feel when I walked the earth. I am not asking you not to feel anger; I am warning you not to give in to your anger. Do not allow anyone to provoke you to compromise your character. Bitterness is the bait of Satan. If you bite his bait and internalize your anger, you will become bitter. Nothing good can be birthed out of bitterness. Come to Me as King David did and pour out your angry heart to Me. Your anger will turn into amazing grace for those who have caused you pain.

Your Lord,
who knows how you feel

*Be angry and do not sin; do not let
the sun go down on your anger, and
give no opportunity to the devil.*

EPHESIANS 4:26–27 ESV

Dear Brother,

I pray you will be like our heavenly Father, who is slow to anger and abounding in steadfast love. May you bless those who curse you and pray for those who persecute you. I pray you will place your hurts and offenses in the hands of your God. May you be calmed and comforted by His presence. May the Holy Spirit give you kind words to say in trying situations, and may you listen to His warnings. I pray you will lay down whatever bitterness you might be holding on to so you can live without that heavy burden. It is in the Father's hands now, and He will give justice.

In Jesus' name,
Amen

My Son,

Sometimes I will allow trials and tribulations in your life to draw you closer to Me, to strengthen you, and to prepare you for battle. I prepared My chosen king David while he was running for his life and hiding in caves. I blinded My apostle Paul until he was ready to see life with My sight. I allowed Job to lose everything so he would know I am all he would ever need in this world. All the sovereign suffering of My chosen warriors led them to the purposeful life that I planned for them. Just as I was with Daniel in the lions' den, I am with you in every trial. You are being prepared for your purpose right now.

Your King,
  who suffers with you

CONSIDER IT PURE JOY, MY BROTHERS AND
SISTERS, WHENEVER YOU FACE TRIALS OF
MANY KINDS, BECAUSE YOU KNOW THAT
THE TESTING OF YOUR FAITH PRODUCES
PERSEVERANCE. LET PERSEVERANCE FINISH
ITS WORK SO THAT YOU MAY BE MATURE AND
COMPLETE, NOT LACKING ANYTHING.

JAMES 1:2–4 TNIV

Dear Brother,

I pray you will find God in your trials. May you see His hand in everything and trust Him completely to pull you through what may seem like a hopeless situation. I pray your faith will be strengthened by the various troubles of this life. May you hold tighter to your Father as the storms hit harder, because He is your Rock and He will never let you fall. I pray you will truly see yourself as His beloved son and trust that He knows what is best for you.

In Jesus' name,
Amen

BE ON GUARD! TURN BACK FROM EVIL,

FOR GOD SENT THIS SUFFERING

TO KEEP YOU FROM A LIFE OF EVIL.

....

JOB 36:21

You are tempted in the same way that everyone else is tempted. But God can be trusted not to let you be tempted too much, and he will show you how to escape from your temptations.

1 CORINTHIANS 10:13 CEV

A WAY OF ESCAPE

My Son,

Spiritual warfare is not a game; it is very real. Sometimes when you feel your strength fading, you will need to run away from temptations to keep from falling. No temptation can conquer you if you get out while there is still time. The enemy will always try to tempt you to linger long enough to entangle you in sin. His strategy has taken down many great men of Mine. I will not allow you to be tempted more than you can handle, and I will always make a way of escape. But only you can ultimately make the choice to take My exit and save yourself from heartache and regret.

Your King,
  your great escape

Because of his glory and excellence, he has given us great and precious promises. These are the promises that enable you to share his divine nature and escape the world's corruption caused by human desires.

2 PETER 1:4

Dear Brother,

I pray you will always rely on your heavenly Father to be your way of escape. He knows the trials you are going through, and He is right there beside you every step of the way. He will not give you more than you can overcome. May you turn to Him in your time of need and let Him show you the way out, a way He has already prepared for you. May you be stronger after each challenge and ready to defeat the next one. I pray you will flee from temptation, cling to righteousness, and be the one who pushes through the dark forces to the light.

In Jesus' name,

Amen

HE WHO DOES NOT TAKE UP HIS CROSS AND
FOLLOW ME IS NOT WORTHY OF ME. HE WHO
FINDS HIS LIFE WILL LOSE IT, AND HE WHO
LOSES HIS LIFE FOR MY SAKE WILL FIND IT.
....
MATTHEW 10:38–39 NKJV

My Son,

I have great and mighty works for you to conquer, but they will be accomplished only if you are willing to deny yourself and your desires and let go of everything and anything to follow Me. I know that what I ask of you is not an easy choice to make; however, the benefits and blessings are great for those who lay down their own desires and dreams to live for Me. Great men of Mine are measured not by how much they can pick up but rather by how much they can lay down. When you are ready to lay down your own life so someone else can live, you truly find the fullness of life.

Your Lord,
  who gave His life for you

THEN JESUS SAID TO HIS DISCIPLES,
"WHOEVER WANTS TO BE MY DISCIPLE
MUST DENY THEMSELVES AND TAKE UP
THEIR CROSS AND FOLLOW ME."

....

MATTHEW 16:24 TNIV

Dear Brother,

May you choose your Lord over yourself every day. I pray that when you feel tempted to try to do anything in your own strength, you will remember what Jesus said: "He who finds his life will lose it, but he who loses his life for My sake will find it." May you lose your own desires and strength so you can line yourself up with His desires and receive His strength. I pray that you will not live for this world but for eternity so you may bring glory to the One who called you His son. May you find a life more abundant in Christ than what you had before.

In Jesus' name,
  Amen

My Son,

Who do you say I am? If I am your great and mighty God, then consider that you were created in My image. If you believe I am who I say I am, then you can believe you are who I say you are. You need nothing from this world to prove your worth but a life lived for My glory, not your own. The praise of men is not enough to fill you up. It will leave you hollow and dry and thirsty for something more. I am the one who will give you the satisfying self-assurance you're searching for. Lose yourself in Me and you will walk in an unshakable confidence and become completely secure.

Your King,
  who defines you

*Out of all the peoples on the face of
the earth, the Lord has chosen you
to be his treasured possession.*

....

DEUTERONOMY 14:2 NIV

Dear Brother,

I pray you will know how highly your Father thinks of you. May you feel His love and acceptance every day. I pray you will treat yourself as an irreplaceable jewel, because that is how the Lord sees you. May you not settle for anything less than you are worth, and may you see yourself the way God sees you . . . perfect in His eyes. I pray you will never allow anyone to tell you who you are except for your heavenly Father, who knows the real you. May you shine for Him.

In Jesus' name,
Amen

But you are a chosen generation, a royal priesthood, a holy nation, His [God's] own special people, that you may proclaim the praises of Him who called you out of darkness into His marvelous light.

1 PETER 2:9 NKJV

"For I know the plans I have for you," says the Lord. "They are plans for good and not for disaster, to give you a future and a hope."

JEREMIAH 29:11

HOPELESSNESS IS AN ILLUSION

My Son,

I am your hope and your mighty God. Just as I parted the Red Sea of hopelessness for Moses and My chosen people, I will part any sea that is blocking you from your freedom. Hopelessness is just an illusion. Don't allow an illusion to become reality. The enemy's fires will not burn you out; raging waters cannot drown your dreams. I am bigger than any challenge you are facing. Fight the temptations to give up and quit. I know the plans I have for you, and they are not for your harm but for your good. I am working on your behalf right now. Trust Me and watch My faithfulness be proven once again!

Your King,
  your hope

Lord, sustain me as you
promised, that I may live!
Do not let my hope be crushed.

PSALM 119:116

Dear Brother,

I pray you may place your hope fully in the Lord who has created you and saved you. He has never let you down and never will. May you feel Him in your darkest times and see Him push things out of the way so you can finish your race strong. I pray that no matter how bad your circumstance is now, you will have hope for the future. May you be sustained by the Lord's promises and be shielded from the evil of this world as you choose daily to put your hope in Him.

In Jesus' name,
Amen

My Son,

When you feel too beaten down to fight,
I want you to give all you have. Stand. Be
strong and keep your faith, no matter what
hits you. You may feel shaken and disoriented
when the enemy assaults you, but I will sup-
ply you with the strength to withstand any
punch. Even when everyone else around you
has been burned-out and struck down by the
pressure of battle, I want you to stand. Be the
man who stands in the gap for those who cannot stand on their own. You wear My armor
and are fully equipped to remain strong until
this spiritual war is finally over and we can
celebrate our victories together.

Your King,
  who stands in for you

SO PUT ON ALL OF GOD'S ARMOR.
EVIL DAYS WILL COME.
BUT YOU WILL BE ABLE TO STAND
UP TO ANYTHING.
AND AFTER YOU HAVE DONE EVERYTHING
YOU CAN, YOU WILL STILL BE STANDING.

EPHESIANS 6:13 NIrV

Dear Brother,

I pray that when the hard days come and
everyone else is falling around you, you may
discover how strong your Father has made
you. I pray you will stand and pull others up
with you. May you never know defeat and
never collapse under pressure, because your
strength to stand is in your Savior, Jesus. You
will be victorious over every evil thing that
comes against you in the name of Jesus. You
will not go down or surrender, because you
were designed to be a conqueror and to succeed. May you stand strong by the grace of
your loving Father.

In Jesus' name,
Amen

MOSES TOLD THE PEOPLE, "DON'T BE AFRAID. JUST STAND STILL AND WATCH THE LORD RESCUE YOU TODAY. THE EGYPTIANS YOU SEE TODAY WILL NEVER BE SEEN AGAIN."

....

EXODUS 14:13

Do all that you can to live in peace with everyone. Dear friends, never take revenge. Leave that to the righteous anger of God. For the Scriptures say, "I will take revenge; I will pay them back," says the LORD.

ROMANS 12:18–19

My Son,

Your fight is not against flesh and blood but against spiritual forces of darkness. Therefore, do not drain your strength trying to prove your point, win your way, or defend yourself to another person. I am your defense. No one ever wins the blame game, so do not engage in it. You are called to live above a life of excuses. Defeat the enemy by fighting for the relationship and doing what you can to bring peace to the situation. The truth is that nothing can stop My plans from coming to pass. Fight for the things worth fighting for—righteousness, salvation, and My name.

Your King,
  your defense

Have nothing to do with foolish,
ignorant controversies; you
know they breed quarrels.

2 TIMOTHY 2:23 ESV

Dear Brother,

I pray you will not exhaust yourself with useless arguments but instead focus on your greater purpose—loving God and loving others. May you be blessed with the strength to walk away from distracting fights and place them in the hands of your Father. He knows who is right and who is wrong, and that is all that matters. I pray you will see the bigger picture and push past relationships that stop you from being all God wants you to be. May you care more about a person's salvation than being right. I pray you will be filled with your Father's grace and love in every difficult relationship you encounter.

In Jesus' name,
Amen

WHATEVER YOU HAVE SAID IN THE DARK
WILL BE HEARD IN THE LIGHT, AND
WHAT YOU HAVE WHISPERED BEHIND
CLOSED DOORS WILL BE SHOUTED FROM
THE HOUSETOPS FOR ALL TO HEAR!
....
LUKE 12:3

IN THE DARK

My Son,

I created you to be a light in the dark places
of this world. Where light is, darkness cannot be. Give Me access to those dark, hidden
places in your heart, and let My marvelous
light penetrate your innermost being. Nothing you have done can be hidden from Me. I
want to eliminate the shame and guilt you feel
for what you have done. Don't waste another
day in shadows; confess your sin to Me. I am
your Redeemer. I will once again set you up
as My light in this dark world. It's time, My
chosen one, to come clean and let your Savior
set you free once again.

Your King,
  who gave for your freedom

YOU ARE THE LIGHT OF THE WORLD—LIKE A CITY ON A HILLTOP THAT CANNOT BE HIDDEN. NO ONE LIGHTS A LAMP AND THEN PUTS IT UNDER A BASKET. INSTEAD, A LAMP IS PLACED ON A STAND, WHERE IT GIVES LIGHT TO EVERYONE IN THE HOUSE.

....

MATTHEW 5:14–15

Dear Brother,

I pray you will live your life in the light with clean hands and a pure heart. May you not try to hide your deeds from your Father. I pray you will have the strength to live your life worthy of being seen. May you let down your pride and confess what you have done in the dark so you do not have to live that way anymore. I pray that you will not be held down by anything from your old life but that you will be held up by the arms of grace in your new, redeemed life in Christ.

In Jesus' name,
Amen

My Son,

I call you "warrior" because I created you in My image. I captivated the world with My tender love and mercy when I walked the earth. I proved My love by serving people to the point of dying on the cross. I called you to follow Me, and I have prepared your heart to love as passionately as I have loved you. It is not enough to fight for your faith. Your tender love for others will make you a true hero. I have given you the power to leave an indelible mark on the hearts of all who are close to you. When this life is over, all that will matter is that you loved well and finished strong.

Your King,
who loved you with His life

Surround me with your tender
mercies so I may live,
for your instructions are my delight.

PSALM 119:77

Dear Brother,

I pray that you, as a tender warrior, will be conscious of every word that comes out of your mouth and every look you give others. May you always have in the forefront of your mind that you are representing your loving Father. I pray you will be drawn toward kindness always, answering each person with grace. May you be softened and broken for others, and may you stay humble in your daily life. I pray you will not hinder the love of Christ from shining through you.

In Jesus' name,
Amen

*The LORD is like a father to his children,
tender and compassionate to those who
fear him. For he knows how weak we
are; he remembers we are only dust.*

PSALM 103:13–14

A time to love and a time to hate.
A time for war and a time for peace.

ECCLESIASTES 3:8

A TIME FOR WAR

My Son,

Right now there is a time of war upon you.
The enemy's attacks are great. It is time for
My people to put on My full armor and
fight like never before. I know the battles you
face will not be easy, but they will be worth
fighting. You will be fighting for your family
and your children's children. Look around;
you are much needed on the battlefield.
Enlist your life in My mighty spiritual army,
and you will not be defeated. There is nothing for you to fear, for I am with you, fighting
for you. You will conquer and win souls for
My kingdom.

Your King,
  who has already won

But all who are able to bear arms
will cross over to fight for the
Lord, *just as you have said.*

NUMBERS 32:27

Dear Brother,

I pray you are aware of the urgent times
before you and ready for what lies ahead.
May you prepare yourself daily by spending
time with the Lord. I pray that you will be
stronger each new day spent in His Word.
I pray that you will not be overwhelmed by
the coming battles but that you will be ready
and victorious. May you equip yourself with
your Father's armor that was designed for
you for such a time as this. I pray a blessing of
strength and endurance and victory over you.

In Jesus' name,
Amen

My Son,

You are not of this world; your citizenship is in heaven. I warn you as a temporary resident to keep away from worldly desires that wage war against your very soul. Don't trade eternal rewards for a life of lust and luxury. I can provide more satisfaction for you than you could ever provide for yourself. Why waste your life storing up treasures here on this earth? I brought you into this life with nothing, and that is how you will leave. Invest your time and talents in the eternal things that will last. Store up your treasures in heaven.

Your Lord,
the builder of your eternal home

JESUS ANSWERED, "MY KINGDOM IS NOT AN EARTHLY KINGDOM. IF IT WERE, MY FOLLOWERS WOULD FIGHT TO KEEP ME FROM BEING HANDED OVER TO THE JEWISH LEADERS. BUT MY KINGDOM IS NOT OF THIS WORLD."

JOHN 18:36

Dear Brother,

I pray you will remember to live your life for the next world. May you store up your treasures in heaven and yet live here on earth in humility and love. I pray that when you are dissatisfied with your home here, you will turn your eyes to heaven and your heavenly Father, who is preparing a better place for you for all eternity. May you not live your life for temporary pleasures and things but only for an everlasting life in heaven. I pray you will find complete comfort in knowing that the best is yet to come.

In Jesus' name,
Amen

DEAR FRIENDS, I WARN YOU AS "TEMPORARY
RESIDENTS AND FOREIGNERS" TO KEEP
AWAY FROM WORLDLY DESIRES THAT WAGE
WAR AGAINST YOUR VERY SOULS.

....

1 PETER 2:11

But now I said to them, "You know very well what trouble we are in. Jerusalem lies in ruins, and its gates have been destroyed by fire. Let us rebuild the wall of Jerusalem and end this disgrace!"

NEHEMIAH 2:17

REBUILD WHAT IS BROKEN

My Son,

I have called you to look to the future with hope and to rebuild what is broken. I am the same God who gave Nehemiah the strength and favor to rebuild the broken walls of Jerusalem, and I will give you the power and strength to do the same. Let Me give you the tools to rebuild broken hearts with words of hope, rebuild broken relationships with forgiveness and grace, rebuild broken cities with selfless service, and rebuke the enemy's lies with words of truth. Begin the building process today by laying one stone of good works at a time.

Your King,
your Master Builder

*I will bring Judah and Israel back
from captivity and will rebuild
them as they were before.*

JEREMIAH 33:7 NIV

Dear Brother,

May you be filled with the power of the Spirit to reshape and rebuild all the broken things around you. I pray you will not be overwhelmed by the task at hand but will be strengthened and encouraged by what your Father has already done. May you feel privileged to be chosen by Him to be His hands and feet. I pray you will step up, help rebuild ruined lives around you, and spread your Savior's love.

In Jesus' name,
Amen

JESUS SAID, "COME TO ME, ALL OF YOU
WHO ARE WEARY AND CARRY HEAVY
BURDENS, AND I WILL GIVE YOU REST."
....
MATTHEW 11:28

REST FOR THE WARRIOR

My Son,

I created a day of rest for My people from the beginning. Rest is not an option; it is a command for My chosen ones. Even I, the Creator of the universe, took a day of rest. I know there are things you want to accomplish, but without restoration you will not have the strength. Don't allow the cares of this world to cause you to become weak and weary. Come to Me and I will give you rest. Lay down your burdens and I will carry them. Rest is My gift to you to renew your strength and refresh your soul. Place your cares in My trustworthy hands, and rest.

Your God,
  your perfect peace

AND GOD BLESSED THE SEVENTH DAY
AND DECLARED IT HOLY, BECAUSE IT
WAS THE DAY WHEN HE RESTED FROM
ALL HIS WORK OF CREATION.
....
GENESIS 2:3

Dear Brother,

I pray you will know the Lord as your refuge
and your comfort. May you lay your burdens
at His feet, and may you be refreshed from
the world by His love. I pray you will stand
on His promise and find rest in your Savior,
Jesus Christ. Let the One who created you
comfort and restore you from the troubles of
this world. I pray the peace of knowing that
the Creator of everything loves you will be
a reality to you. May you be strengthened in
Him so you will be ready for your next battle.

In Jesus' name,
Amen

CONQUER EVIL

My Son,

The enemy will try to persuade you to conquer evil with evil, but if you give in, you will lose every time. You never need to give in to the temptation to conquer evil by responding with evil. That tactic is for the weak. Remember that revenge brings nothing but pain, destruction, and regret. It is love that brings peace, healing, and My blessing. My Spirit is in you; therefore, you have the inner strength to love at any cost. Be extreme, and love others most when they deserve it the least . . . the way I love you!

Your Lord,
  who loved you with His life

Instead,
"If your enemies are hungry, feed them.
If they are thirsty, give them
something to drink.
In doing this, you will heap
burning coals of shame on their heads."
Don't let evil conquer you, but
conquer evil by doing good.

ROMANS 12:20–21

Dear Brother,

I pray you will rely on the strength of God to love your enemies and bless those who curse you. May you be not be distracted or angered by the wrongdoings of your enemies but instead be full of grace and love. May others—including your enemies—see the light of Jesus in you, and may they be directed toward our God by your example of His love. I pray you will be faithful to this truth even in the hardest times. No righteous act is unseen by the Lord; you will be victorious and blessed for your obedience.

In Jesus' name,
Amen

I tell you: Love your enemies and pray for those who persecute you, that you may be sons of your Father in heaven.

MATTHEW 5:44–45 NIV

Then Joshua told the people,
"Purify yourselves,
for tomorrow the LORD will do
great wonders among you."

JOSHUA 3:5

THE POWER OF PURITY

My Son,

It is time to purify yourself. With every temptation the enemy fires at you, you have a choice. You can cave to your craving for temporary pleasures and destroy your soul, or you can call to Me so I will make a way for you to escape. I am a holy God, and I want you to live a life of holiness. I am not asking for perfection, but I am asking for your purity to be a priority in your life. Remove from your path anything that causes you to stumble and fall away from Me. It is purity that will give you peace of mind. Your purity will bring My promises to pass in your life.

Your King,
  who purifies you

Blessed are the pure in heart,
for they will see God.

MATTHEW 5:8 NIV

Dear Brother,

I pray you will purify yourself before the Lord so you can be in His presence. May everything you do be of sound spirit and righteous actions and pleasing to the Lord. May you stand out among the impurity in this world. In order to make a difference, you must be different. May you have the strength and wisdom to choose the life your Father has placed before you, and may you say no to the snare of impurity set by Satan. I pray that by your pure actions, the world will be certain you are a child of the King. May you live purely by listening to His Spirit.

In Jesus' name,
Amen

My Son,

No matter where you've gone or what you've done or said, I have covered you with My blood. If you refuse to forgive yourself, you are saying My death on the cross was not enough to set you free from sin. At the cross I covered your guilt, your shame, your regret, and your pain. I washed you clean with My blood. I cover you every day with My extravagant love and mercy. My grace is a free gift. Take this gift and give it away to those who have let you down or disappointed you. Amazing grace is a reflection of My love for the world to see through you.

Your God,
  your grace

BUT MY LIFE IS WORTH NOTHING TO ME
UNLESS I USE IT FOR FINISHING THE WORK
ASSIGNED ME BY THE LORD JESUS—THE
WORK OF TELLING OTHERS THE GOOD NEWS
ABOUT THE WONDERFUL GRACE OF GOD.

....
ACTS 20:24

Dear Brother,

I pray you will fully understand the grace your Father has given you, as only He can cover your past and make you new again. May you find peace and shelter in the coverings of His abundant love and grace. Nothing can separate you from Him if you continue to obey Him, so I pray you will obey His commands and keep yourself under His protection. May you be safe from the evil in this world, and live in abundant blessing.

In Jesus' name,
Amen

FINALLY, I CONFESSED ALL MY SINS TO YOU
AND STOPPED TRYING TO HIDE MY GUILT.
I SAID TO MYSELF, "I WILL CONFESS
MY REBELLION TO THE LORD."
AND YOU FORGAVE ME! ALL MY GUILT IS GONE.

....

PSALM 32:5

Entering [the adulterous woman's] house leads to death; it is the road to the grave. The man who visits her is doomed. He will never reach the paths of life. Follow the steps of good men instead, and stay on the paths of the righteous.

PROVERBS 2:18–20

My Son,

I created a woman to complete a man. Yet My beautiful creation has been used too many times by the enemy to cripple. There are immoral women who will destroy the foundation I built for families. Too many of My mighty men have not guarded their hearts and minds and have fallen prey to the seduction of this kind of woman in a moment of weakness. Do not think you are strong enough to handle the seduction of such a woman. Run from her. I will make a way for you to escape. But you must choose to take My way out.

Your Father,
  your escape

For why should you, my son, be enraptured by an immoral woman, and be embraced in the arms of a seductress? For the ways of man are before the eyes of the LORD, *and He ponders all his paths.*

PROVERBS 5:20–21 NKJV

Dear Brother,

I pray you will view each woman as your sister in Christ. May you not become entangled in a seducing trap of the enemy. I pray you will be a faithful man, able to withstand temptations that can tear you apart if you choose them. May the way you live your life show purity in yourself and therefore inspire purity in those around you. May you reflect the respectful, loving gaze of Jesus every time you look at a woman, and may you build her up and protect her decency with all your thoughts and actions.

In Jesus' name,
Amen

PAUL AND SILAS WERE PRAYING AND SINGING HYMNS TO GOD, AND THE PRISONERS WERE LISTENING TO THEM. SUDDENLY, THERE WAS A GREAT EARTHQUAKE, SO THAT THE FOUNDATIONS OF THE PRISONS WERE SHAKEN; AND IMMEDIATELY ALL THE DOORS WERE OPENED AND EVERYONE'S CHAINS WERE LOOSED.

ACTS 16:25–26 NKJV

PRAISE THROUGH THE PAIN

My Son,

Pain is inevitable in this fallen world. But I have given you the strength to endure anything the enemy attempts to do to torment you. I can use hurtful situations to make you into the man I created you to be. I want you to learn to praise Me in pain and to become a comfort to others. Your praise will become the keys to your freedom. Your praise will call down heaven to earth, and I will move mightily in your life if you will praise Me during difficult times. If you trust Me, then praise Me until I come to your rescue. I will do whatever it takes for your freedom.

Your King,
  who frees you

HE HAS GIVEN ME A NEW SONG TO SING, A
HYMN OF PRAISE TO OUR GOD. MANY WILL
SEE WHAT HE HAS DONE AND BE AMAZED.
THEY WILL PUT THEIR TRUST IN THE LORD.
....

PSALM 40:3

Dear Brother,

God is always good, and I pray you will know how worthy He is of your praise all the time. May you give uninhibited and unashamed praise to your heavenly Father. May darkness be brought into the light, and may chains be broken by your pure worship and praise to the Lord. I pray you will find the strength to praise Him even when you feel too weak to give anything. May you give all that you have to Him and receive His endless blessings as you offer praise to your Lord.

In Jesus' name,
Amen

My Son,

You were born to lead. But only you can make
the choice to step into your appointed position as a leader. You are called to raise the bar
and bring others up; do not allow them to
bring you down. No matter what choice you
make, you will lead others by your example—
good or bad. Your obedience to Me is the
only weapon that will destroy the works of
the enemy in your life. I will go before you
and prepare the way. In My power you will
have the wisdom and influence needed to
become a great leader. Walk in My confidence, not your own, and lead My people.

Your King,
  who leads you

Now go, for I am sending you to Pharaoh. You must lead my people Israel out of Egypt.

EXODUS 3:10

Dear Brother,

I pray you will become ready and equipped to lead others with your life. May you serve anyone anywhere, just as Jesus did while He walked this earth. May you be humble and receive the wisdom that comes from fearing the Lord and listening to His voice. I pray you will not attempt to tackle problems in your own strength but will rely fully on your heavenly Father. I pray that your obedience will bring you favor in this world, enabling you to influence people everywhere you go, spreading the goodness of God.

In Jesus' name,
Amen

Israel's leaders took charge,
and the people gladly followed.
Praise the LORD!

....

JUDGES 5:2

So do not throw away this confident trust in the Lord. Remember the great reward it brings you! Patient endurance is what you need now, so that you will continue to do God's will. Then you will receive all that he has promised.

HEBREWS 10:35–36

My Son,

I ask you on this day, "Whom do you trust?"
I am the author of your life, and I am the
giver of every breath you take. I want you
to surrender all fear to Me and to trust Me.
Remember, I hold in My mighty hand all of
your tomorrows. They were laid out before
you were born. Give up the fight in your own
mind of trying to figure it all out. Don't let
your circumstances hold your heart hostage
or cause you to lose your confidence in Me.
So I am asking you today to answer this one
question: "In whom do you place your trust?"

Your trustworthy King,
    who loves you

But those who trust in the Lord
will find new strength.
They will soar high on wings like eagles.
They will run and not grow weary.
They will walk and not faint.

ISAIAH 40:31

Dear Brother,

I pray you will put your trust fully in the One who knows everything and created everything, including you. May you trust that your heavenly Father knows what is best for you and that He will work everything out for your good. He is not going to tell everyone your secrets and insecurities, and He will not mock your fears. He is love, and He will protect you. I pray you will lay down whatever you are holding on to that is making you uneasy or ineffective. May you leave it at His feet.

In Jesus' name,
   Amen

THE WORKFORCE

My Son,

I am the God who gave you the ability to work, and wherever you work is your mission field. There is so much more to your job than profit and status. What do you profit if you gain everything and lose your soul? Your work ethic is a reflection of Me. I have destined you for success. You do not have to give in to the work ethic of this world. Pursue a spirit of excellence in everything you do. Do your work as unto Me, and in My time I will reward you greatly for glorifying Me in the workforce.

Your God,
whose rewards are great

FOR GOD IS NOT UNJUST TO FORGET YOUR
WORK AND LABOR OF LOVE WHICH YOU HAVE
SHOWN TOWARD HIS NAME, IN THAT YOU HAVE
MINISTERED TO THE SAINTS, AND DO MINISTER.

HEBREWS 6:10 NKJV

Dear Brother,

May the Lord's favor be upon you in your place of work. I pray you will work as if you were working only for God Himself. May you glorify Him in everything you do and say. I pray that you will respond to every situation at work with integrity and grace and that you will set the standard of principles. May you be blessed in all your endeavors, and may all your efforts be greatly multiplied and fruitful so the Lord will be glorified.

In Jesus' name,
Amen

LIVE SUCH GOOD LIVES AMONG THE PAGANS
THAT, THOUGH THEY ACCUSE YOU OF DOING
WRONG, THEY MAY SEE YOUR GOOD DEEDS
AND GLORIFY GOD ON THE DAY HE VISITS US.

1 PETER 2:12 NIV

If you fully obey the LORD your God and carefully follow all his commands I give you today, the LORD your God will set you high above all the nations on earth. All these blessings will come on you and accompany you if you obey the LORD your God.

DEUTERONOMY 28:1–2 NIV

My Son,

It is your time to break free from mediocrity and break through to the life of abundant blessing and adventure. I have handed you the keys to unlock a life better than you could ever hope for, but I will not force you to live for Me. Obedience is a choice only you can make. If you choose My will over your way, I will bless your obedience by allowing you to prosper in everything you do that brings glory to Me. Your obedient life will release My blessing and favor not only on you but also on your family and many generations to follow.

Your King,
  your blessing

The LORD will send a blessing on your barns and on everything you put your hand to. The LORD your God will bless you in the land he is giving you.

DEUTERONOMY 28:8 NIV

Dear Brother,

I pray you will experience the fullness of
blessings from obedience to the Lord. I pray
you will honor and fear Him as you make
every decision, knowing that each choice
you make has a consequence. I pray you will
always choose obedience, even when it is the
hardest thing to do. May you be the one who
paves the way for your children and grand-
children to live righteous lives, free from the
bondage and consequences of their parents'
sin. May you be holy and pure in everything
you do and set an example to other believers
of how a child of God is supposed to live.

In Jesus' name,
Amen

YET GOD HAS MADE EVERYTHING BEAUTIFUL
FOR ITS OWN TIME. HE HAS PLANTED
ETERNITY IN THE HUMAN HEART, BUT EVEN
SO, PEOPLE CANNOT SEE THE WHOLE SCOPE
OF GOD'S WORK FROM BEGINNING TO END.
....
ECCLESIASTES 3:11

My Son,

Live your life driven by eternity. Don't waste your days pouring your heart and soul into things that will not make an undying impact. Do not let your faith be shaken by a bad day. What is one day compared to eternity? Remember to look at the big picture. If you will let the blaze of eternity burn in your heart, you will be more than a light in the darkness; your faith will be a contagious fire sparking faith in people all around you. Your life lived for Me will become a legacy that will still be effective in the hearts of men long after you're gone. Greatness is yours when eternity reigns on earth through you.

Your King,
   who loves you for all eternity

THEY SHARE FREELY AND GIVE
GENEROUSLY TO THOSE IN NEED.
THEIR GOOD DEEDS WILL BE
REMEMBERED FOREVER.
THEY WILL HAVE INFLUENCE AND HONOR.
....

PSALM 112:9

Dear Brother,

I pray you will live a life that directs people toward Jesus. May all you do be a godly example to others, and may they desire more of the Father by the faithful way you live your life. I pray you will do each act of kindness as if you were doing it directly to Jesus Himself. May you give all for the Lord, holding nothing back, and may you be blessed for your work. I pray you will have the strength to love the unlovable, forgive the unforgiveable, and live for that glorious day when you hear, "Well done, good and faithful servant."

In Jesus' name,
Amen

My Son,

You never need to compromise your character to get ahead. You are set apart and called to live a life reflecting that you are Mine. If you fully trust Me, you will find the strength to conquer compromise. What matters most to Me is what you do when only I am watching. I am the one who sees your heart. Your choice to walk with Me on the narrow road will give you so much more than the wide road that leads to a life of dishonor and destruction. Live your life according to My standards, not your own, and I will give you the desires of your heart.

Your Lord,
   who does not compromise

They do not compromise with evil,
and they walk only in his paths.
You have charged us to keep your
commandments carefully.

....

PSALM 119:3–4

Dear Brother,

May you never sacrifice the many blessings God has for you for temporary pleasure. I pray you have divine wisdom, always able to discern the forces of darkness that wage war against your soul. May you live with strong conviction by the power of God, knowing you are set apart for His divine purpose. I pray you will rest in His everlasting love and see all His promises come to pass in your life because of your obedience.

In Jesus' name,
Amen

Keep watch and pray, so that you will not give in to temptation. For the spirit is willing, but the body is weak.

....

MATTHEW 26:41

But seek first his kingdom and his righteousness, and all these things will be given to you as well. Therefore do not worry about tomorrow, for tomorrow will worry about itself. Each day has enough trouble of its own.

MATTHEW 6:33–34 NIV

CAPTURE THIS DAY

My Son,

The enemy of your soul wants to torment you with worry and fear of the future. This is a disruptive trap set by Satan himself. Do not waste your strength today, fighting to figure out tomorrow. Capture this day. If you take your eyes off today, you will grow weary from worry. Don't you know by now that I hold all your tomorrows in My hands? I will never let you down. Today is My gift to you—open it and live it passionately for Me. I am asking you on this day to be where you are and give all you have right now. I want you to stop worrying about your future and focus on your faith in Me. Let this day be one well lived.

Your King,
  who made this day

This is the day the Lord has made.
We will rejoice and be glad in it.

PSALM 118:24

Dear Brother,

I pray you will take this day that the Lord has given you and live it to the fullest. May you not waste your time or your Father's time by doing your own thing; instead, take this day and give it back to God. I pray you will be blind to the useless worries of the future. May you not worry about tomorrow but devote yourself only to the day right in front of you. May your efforts be multiplied, and may you be productive and efficient for the kingdom this very day.

In Jesus' name,
Amen

My Son,

There are unseen spiritual battles going on
all around you. You must learn to fight in the
power of My Spirit, not with your human
flesh. My Holy Spirit will be your sight when
you cannot see the invisible attacks fired at
you. Your faith in Me is your shield when you
feel oppressed by the enemy, and My Word is
your sword to strike down your opponents.
Do not fear, My son—you are fully equipped
to fight the good fight of your faith. I will
not let you live a life of defeat. You can take
authority over darkness. I will give you the
power to triumph over every trial.

Your King,
   who has already won

FOR OUR STRUGGLE IS NOT AGAINST FLESH AND
BLOOD, BUT AGAINST THE RULERS, AGAINST
THE AUTHORITIES, AGAINST THE POWERS OF
THIS DARK WORLD AND AGAINST THE SPIRITUAL
FORCES OF EVIL IN THE HEAVENLY REALMS.

EPHESIANS 6:12 NIV

Dear Brother,

I pray you will walk in the authority Jesus has given you in His name over the darkness and evil of this world. May you be triumphant in every encounter you have with the enemy, and may God be glorified in your victories. I pray you are able to discern and fight the enemy as a chosen warrior of the almighty God. May you have peace in knowing that, though you cannot see them, your God will send angels to surround you and lift you up. May you be strengthened in that knowledge and in His presence.

In Jesus' name,
Amen

YOU USED TO LIVE IN SIN, JUST LIKE THE REST OF THE WORLD, OBEYING THE DEVIL—THE COMMANDER OF THE POWERS IN THE UNSEEN WORLD. HE IS THE SPIRIT AT WORK IN THE HEARTS OF THOSE WHO REFUSE TO OBEY GOD.

EPHESIANS 2:2

I am the L<small>ORD</small> *All-Powerful. So don't depend on your own power or strength, but on my Spirit.*

ZECHARIAH 4:6 CEV

My Son,

It doesn't matter how strong or fast or clever you are on the outside. Apart from Me you are powerless. You must learn to fight your enemy in My strength, not yours. If you do not let My strength flow through you, then you will not win. The enemy jabs at your weak spots, but you can overtake him in My authority. Be strong in your faith, and fight with the weapon of My Word and the power of prayer. Don't go another round with the evil one in your own strength, and don't sit down in weary defeat. Step back into to the ring and fight like the man of God I have trained you to be . . . and you will win.

Your Lord,
  your victory

I am the vine, you are the branches. He who abides in Me, and I in him, bears much fruit; for without Me you can do nothing.

JOHN 15:5 NKJV

Dear Brother,

I pray you will be filled with the power of
the Holy Spirit and not be deceived by the
enemy into thinking you can do battle in your
own strength. May you always be aware that
apart from God, you can do nothing. I pray
you will stay immersed in His power and in
His strength so you can be successful in the
battles to come. May you take hope in the
knowledge that your loving Father gives His
power freely to those who obey Him and stay
near Him. I pray you will not separate yourself from Him.

In Jesus' name,
Amen

PRAISE THE LORD. BLESSED ARE
THOSE WHO FEAR THE LORD,
WHO FIND GREAT DELIGHT IN HIS COMMANDS.
THEIR CHILDREN WILL BE MIGHTY IN THE LAND;
THE GENERATION OF THE
UPRIGHT WILL BE BLESSED.
WEALTH AND RICHES ARE IN THEIR HOUSES,
AND THEIR RIGHTEOUSNESS ENDURES FOREVER.

PSALM 112:1–3 TNIV

My Son,

If you pay attention to the commands of your Lord, I will abundantly bless you for your obedient heart. I will grant you victory over any enemies who rise up against you. I will send blessings to rain on your household, and I will bless your children because you lived your life according to My standards and not the world's. I will open heaven's storehouse to you so you may bless others with all I give you. I will bless you with peace of mind for your faithfulness. Your life will be one well celebrated because you lived for Me.

Your King,
your blessing

BLESSED ARE THOSE WHO HUNGER AND THIRST
FOR RIGHTEOUSNESS, FOR THEY SHALL BE FILLED.
....

MATTHEW 5:6 NKJV

Dear Brother,

I pray a blessing over you that can be given only by the Lord. May you know that everything you touch and every path you take will be blessed because you have obeyed your Father. May you hold on to His promises and blessings that He has for His children, and may you always be grateful for each new day He gives you. I pray you will continue to fear and obey the Lord by His power.

In Jesus' name,
Amen

RELEASE YOUR PRISONER

My Son,

Forgiveness is not an option; it is My command. I am a just God, and I will deal with those who cause My people pain. Don't allow yourself to remain a prisoner of self-defeat because you won't forgive. I gave My life for your freedom. Take the keys and unlock the prison door that is holding your heart hostage. You can't fight the good fight of faith with heavy chains of bitterness on your ankles. Refusing to forgive is not hurting or hindering anyone but you. Lay down your unforgiving ways at My cross. When you release your prisoner, you release yourself.

Your King,
   who has forgiven you

Even if that person wrongs you seven times a day and each time turns again and asks forgiveness, you must forgive.

....

LUKE 17:4

Dear Brother,

I pray you will take the forgiveness your loving Father has given to you and give it freely to those who have offended you. May you be free from the bondage of bitterness, and may you let God do the judging and punishing of those who have wronged you. I pray you will not let your pride hinder you any longer from the call the Lord has laid out for your life, and I pray you release any refusal to forgive that has been holding you hostage.

In Jesus' name,
Amen

If you forgive those who sin against you,
your heavenly Father will forgive you.

....

MATTHEW 6:14

*Don't trap yourself by making
a rash promise to God
and only later counting the cost.*

PROVERBS 20:25

COUNT THE COST

My Son,

You must count the cost of any and all commitments you make before you make them. Opportunities that may appear good could become a trap set by the enemy to capture your time and talents. You are of great value whether you believe it or not; I want you to spend your time wisely. Take more time to pray and seek Me, and I will reveal what is right for you. Don't allow anyone but Me to move you into a position that requires your time and attention. I am your navigator in this life. Never let anyone guilt you into going places I have not mapped out for you.

Your King,
   who paid the price for you

Christ has set us free to live a free life. So take your stand! Never again let anyone put a harness of slavery on you.

GALATIANS 5:1 MESSAGE

Dear Brother,

I pray you would be wise in your commitments and decision making. May you be able to see all the angles and possibilities, discerning what God's will is for you and not depending only on what seems right to you. I pray that you will humbly seek godly counsel and that you will know that not every open door is of God. May the Lord be gracious to you and show you what He wants you to commit your time to. May you be a man of your word and bring glory to God by your commitments.

In Jesus' name,
Amen

My Son,

Nothing is impossible for Me. All I ask is that you be faithful in the little things. I am your faithful Father who will move mountains for you if you have faith in Me even as small as a mustard seed. I am the one who multiplies fish and bread to feed My children. I sent My Son into the world in the form of a little baby. Greatness begins with the little things you do to glorify Me. I bless whatever you give Me no matter how big or small. Begin your faith walk with the little things and expect to see big miracles happen in your life.

Your Lord,
  who holds nothing back

"YOU DON'T HAVE ENOUGH FAITH," JESUS TOLD THEM. "I TELL YOU THE TRUTH, IF YOU HAD FAITH EVEN AS SMALL AS A MUSTARD SEED, YOU COULD SAY TO THIS MOUNTAIN, 'MOVE FROM HERE TO THERE,' AND IT WOULD MOVE. NOTHING WOULD BE IMPOSSIBLE."

MATTHEW 17:20

Dear Brother,

I pray you will be faithful in all you do. No matter how small a task, may you do it in excellence, because your heavenly Father is watching. He wants you to be faithful with the little things so you can be prepared for the big ones. I pray you will be blessed for your faithfulness with what little you have and be given much more as a reward. May you truly be called a good and faithful servant of the Lord.

In Jesus' name,
Amen

THE MASTER WAS FULL OF PRAISE. "WELL DONE,
MY GOOD AND FAITHFUL SERVANT. YOU HAVE
BEEN FAITHFUL IN HANDLING THIS SMALL
AMOUNT, SO NOW I WILL GIVE YOU MANY MORE
RESPONSIBILITIES. LET'S CELEBRATE TOGETHER!"

MATTHEW 25:21

*Then the king appointed Daniel to
a high position and gave him many
valuable gifts. He made Daniel ruler
over the whole province of Babylon, as
well as chief over all his wise men.*

DANIEL 2:48

TAKE YOUR APPOINTED POSITION

My Son,

Just as I appointed My chosen one Daniel to a high position and gave him many valuable gifts, I, your King, have appointed you as well. Your character and commitment will place you in your true appointed position. There is a hope and a future for you, but only you can capture it by seeking My face with all your heart, mind, and strength. There is a call on your life, but only you can answer it. You must choose for yourself whether you will settle for less than I offer. Now is your time to take your rightful place as a man of faith and to change lives for eternity.

Your King,
who appointed you

I knew you before I formed you
in your mother's womb.
Before you were born I set you apart
and appointed you as my
prophet to the nations.

JEREMIAH 1:5

Dear Brother,

I pray you will not let a day go by without being in the position God has for you. May you find where you are most effective and thrive there in excellence. May you not be distracted by anything that does not place you where you are needed most. I pray you will have a clear-cut vision for your life and not second-guess the will of the Lord, since we know that He works everything out for the good of those who love Him and are called according to His purpose. I pray you will be effective and blessed in your ministry.

In Jesus' name,
Amen

NOW TO HIM WHO IS ABLE TO DO
IMMEASURABLY MORE THAN ALL WE
ASK OR IMAGINE, ACCORDING TO HIS
POWER THAT IS AT WORK WITHIN US.
....
EPHESIANS 3:20 NIV

My Son,

Because you have My Spirit inside you, you have My power to live a life without limits. There is no war I cannot win for you. There is no problem I cannot solve for you. There is no life too broken that I cannot put it back together again. There are no chains strong enough that I cannot break them. Nothing can limit you from living an abundant life but your disobedience and lack of faith. Choose to obey My commands, and you will feel My power and passion inside your soul. I will do immeasurably more than you would ever dare to ask of Me or imagine.

Your King,
who knows no limits

"MY THOUGHTS ARE NOTHING LIKE YOUR THOUGHTS," SAYS THE LORD. "AND MY WAYS ARE FAR BEYOND ANYTHING YOU COULD IMAGINE."

....

ISAIAH 55:8

Dear Brother,

I pray you will be given dreams and vision beyond your comprehension and have the faith to see them through. May you never put your God in a box. May you truly know that nothing is impossible with Him if you are faithful. I pray that He will use you to do things you could never imagine and that you will take the first step by giving your loving Father everything you have to give. May all your adventures with Him be blessed.

In Jesus' name,
Amen

My Son,

Deception is a weapon launched by the enemy to keep the world from finding My truth. But I, your God, will give you access to a greater device—the weapon of wisdom. When you use the weaponry of My Word, you will break down walls and destroy the deceptive works of the enemy. My wisdom will become your guard, your guide, and your gauge to navigate your way through the battlefield. My wisdom will give you the skills to rebuild and restore broken lives, including your own. If you get lost in My Word, you will never be blinded by deception again.

Your King,
  who freely gives wisdom

*For the L*ORD *gives wisdom, and from his mouth come knowledge and understanding. He holds victory in store for the upright. He is a shield to those whose walk is blameless, for he guards the course of the just and protects the way of his faithful ones.*

PROVERBS 2:6–8 NIV

Dear Brother,

I pray you will depend only on the wisdom that comes from God and not trust the false wisdom that comes from man. May you not be deceived by the enemy, forfeiting the wisdom the Lord has freely given you. May you always remember that He alone gives wisdom and from His mouth come knowledge and understanding. May you hold on to His wisdom tightly and use it frequently. I pray your fear of the Lord will indeed be rewarded with wisdom, as He says in His Word. May you be blessed as you make decisions with your Father at your side.

In Jesus' name,
Amen

For wisdom will enter your heart, and knowledge will be pleasant to your soul. Discretion will protect you, and understanding will guard you. Wisdom will save you from the ways of wicked men, from men whose words are perverse.

PROVERBS 2:10–12 NIV

I said to myself, "I will watch what I do
And not sin in what I say.
I will hold my tongue when the
ungodly are around me."

PSALM 39:1

My Son,

Your tongue is a powerful weapon; with it
you build others up or tear them down. You
can bring peace or war with your words. You
can speak with compassion or you can crush
someone's spirit. I have anointed your tongue
to counteract the enemy's verbal attacks on
you and My church. I have chosen you to
be My voice of comfort and courage to the
world. Your words can deliver hope to the
hopeless and life-changing truth to those lost
in lies. Let your words be a blessing, not a
curse. Let them be a reflection of Me every
time you open your mouth to speak.

Your King,
    who is life

Take control of what I say, O Lord,
and guard my lips.

PSALM 141:3

Dear Brother,

I pray that every word you speak and every thought you have will be filled with life and love. May the words you speak change the life of someone who is feeling discouraged or burdened. I pray you will depend on the Lord to control your tongue. I pray you will spend time with Him to know how to speak like Him. I pray you will speak words that bring reconciliation and hope to all who hear them. May your lips speak truth and be blessed by the King so you bring healing to a hurting world.

In Jesus' name,
Amen

THE LEGACY

My Son,

Your life lived for Me will become the legacy that lives on long after you are gone. Your commitment to the call will carve character in the next generation. Every prayer you pray will become a blessing passed down. Every tough choice you make to obey Me will become a foundation your family will stand on in difficult times. Your trust in Me will remain in others who watched you walk in peace. I, your God, declare on this day that your children's children will be forever blessed, because you lived your life for an audience of One . . . Me.

Your King,
who believes in you

HAPPY ARE THOSE WHO DELIGHT IN DOING
WHAT HE COMMANDS. THEIR CHILDREN WILL
BE SUCCESSFUL EVERYWHERE; AN ENTIRE
GENERATION OF GODLY PEOPLE WILL BE BLESSED.
THEY THEMSELVES WILL BE WEALTHY, AND THEIR
GOOD DEEDS WILL NEVER BE FORGOTTEN.

PSALM 112:1–3

Dear Brother,

I pray the blessings you receive will be multi-plied and passed down to your children and your children's children. May you be the one who breaks generational curses and starts generational blessings! May you be known as the one who lived a selfless life full of love. May you be the one who showed people Christ—all because you loved them. I pray you will be the one remembered for your godly counsel and your kind spirit and your undying love for your heavenly Father.

In Jesus' name,
Amen

BUT I LAVISH UNFAILING LOVE FOR A
THOUSAND GENERATIONS ON THOSE WHO
LOVE ME AND OBEY MY COMMANDS.

....

When he had received the drink, Jesus said, "It is finished." With that, he bowed his head and gave up his spirit.

JOHN 19:30 TNIV

IT IS FINISHED!

My Son,

It is finished! I, your Savior, paid the price for your eternal life when I drew My last breath on the cross. I conquered death, I covered your sin with My blood, and I crushed the enemy. My Spirit is in you to finish the work you have been sent to do. My power is yours to use. My keys to freedom are yours to share. My grace is your gift to receive. All regret or guilt is gone, and the new has come. Never doubt how much you are loved—I proved it on the cross. Walk in the truth. It is finished, and you will finish strong.

Your Savior King,
  who loves you more than you can imagine

If you confess with your mouth, "Jesus is Lord," and believe in your heart that God raised him from the dead, you will be saved.

ROMANS 10:9 NIV

Dear Brother,

I pray that you, child of God, know the importance of being in a personal relationship with the Father. May you confess your sins to Him and bring yourself to right standing with your Creator who loves you and wants what is best for you. May you leave your old ways and live in a new life with Christ. May you accept Him fully into your life, knowing that He is your only way to the Father and to eternal life. May you accept the Lord's free gift of grace and live for Him from this day on. May you know the Lord better each day, feel His love, and see Him working on your behalf.

In Jesus' name,
Amen

Jacob A. Shepherd is the founder of Life Inc. Min-
istries and an award-winning communicator. He is a
frequent speaker at Nextgenhusband conferences for
mothers of sons as well as at youth events through-
out the country. Recently he lived and worked for a
year at the Los Angeles Dream Center in the inner
city of Los Angeles, helping to rebuild broken families. He lives
with his beautiful wife, Amanda, in North Carolina.

Sheri Rose Shepherd is the bestselling author of
His Princess: Love Letters from Your King; *His Princess
Bride: Love Letters from Your Prince*; and several
other books. She speaks to tens of thousands of
women every year. Her story has been one of the
most popular shows on *Focus on the Family* and has
also been featured on the *Billy Graham Primetime Television
Special*, seen nationwide.